Photo by Joan Marcus

A scene from the Manhattan Theatre Club production of "By the Sea By the Sea By the Beautiful Sea." Set design by Michael McGarty.

BY THE SEA
BY THE SEA
BY THE
BEAUTIFUL SEA

BY
JOE PINTAURO,
LANFORD WILSON and
TERRENCE McNALLY

★

DRAMATISTS
PLAY SERVICE
INC.

BY THE SEA BY THE SEA BY THE BEAUTIFUL SEA
Copyright © 1996, Joe Pintauro,
Lanford Wilson, and Terrence McNally

ALL RIGHTS RESERVED

SPECIAL NOTE

SPECIAL NOTE ON SONGS AND RECORDINGS

BY THE SEA BY THE SEA BY THE BEAUTIFUL SEA was produced by Manhattan Theatre Club (Lynne Meadow, Artistic Director; Barry Grove, Executive Director) in New York City, in May, 1996. It was directed by Leonard Foglia; the set design was by Michael McGarty; the costume design was by Laura Cunningham; the lighting design was by Brian MacDevitt; the sound design was by One Dream Sound; and the production stage manager was Jill Cordle. The cast was as follows:

DAWN

PAT .... Mary Beth Fisher
VERONICA .... Lee Brock
QUENTIN .... Timothy Carhart

DAY

ACE.. Timothy Carhart
MACY.. Lee Brock
BILL... Mary Beth Fisher

DUSK

DANA .... Mary Beth Fisher
WILLY.. Timothy Carhart
MARSHA .... Lee Brock

BY THE SEA BY THE SEA BY THE BEAUTIFUL SEA received its premiere at Bay Street Theatre (Sybil Christopher, Emma Walton, Artistic Directors; Stephen Hamilton, Executive Director) in Sag Harbor, New York, in July, 1995. It was directed by Leonard Foglia; the set design was by Michael McGarty; the costume design was by Laura Cunningham; the lighting design was by Brian MacDevitt; the sound design was by Randy Freed; and the production stage manager was Linda Barnes. The cast was as follows:

DAWN

PAT	Mary Beth Fisher
VERONICA	Lee Brock
QUENTIN	Holt McCallany

DAY

ACE	Holt McCallany
MACY	Lee Brock
BILL	Mary Beth Fisher

DUSK

DANA	Mary Beth Fisher
WILLY	Holt McCallany
MARSHA	Lee Brock

TABLE OF CONTENTS

SETTING

The nine characters of the trilogy, *By the Sea By the Sea By the Beautiful Sea*, all play out their respective situations at the same ocean beach, on the same day, sometime in August, during the week of the Perseid meteor showers. The audience is, presumably, in the water. There are at least two sandy dunes.

DAWN

CHARACTERS

QUENTIN or "Q" — As his sister Veronica calls him, is a clean cut man nearing forty. He is dressed like the President of the United States: good suit, Barney's dress shirt, black silk tie, new shoes. Formerly a hip and slick lawyer, Quentin has recently turned Republican (he's now a counsel to the Senate Judiciary Committee in D.C.). "Q" puts out a more literate and witty, very upper-middle class aura, but the raging tough guy is still in there somewhere, ready to bite back when things get serious.

VERONICA or "RONNIE" — Quentin's sister. Younger or older doesn't matter. She is one of those witty women who eats chocolates and licks her fingers while doing other things, everything but look at the person to whom she's speaking. She's a sociophobe affecting a defensive, sophisticated ennui, but in her heart, Ronnie is an angel who resorts to cruelty only out of nervous desperation and unbearable loneliness. She'll do anything to evoke a passionate response to soothe deep feelings of invisibility. She is dressed in black. She even wears a black bathing suit.

PATRICIA or "Pat" — Quentin's wife, Veronica's friend and sister-in-law. Here is a high functioning woman of high moral quality. She's a Republican by habit but her values are Democratic. A Smith grad, she tip-toes around the middle class neuroses of her in-laws with a strategy of: "Don't make waves. They'll never get it anyway." When push comes to shove, a strong moral persona emerges. She's a Buddhist and wears white for this solemn occasion.

DAWN

Blackness. The opening two words of Mozart's Requiem,*
"Kyrie Eleison" and a sky full of stars appears. As the mu-
sic crashes, so does an ocean wave, washing over the audi-
ence. As the sounds recede, a woman is heard chanting on
the beach in the dark. It's Pat. She's sitting on a dune chant-
ing "Om Namah Shivayha," the Sanskrit mantra which
means, "I bow to the Lord," traditionally sung at nighttime.
After a moment she switches on a flashlight and continues
chanting in the darkness. She casts the flashlight beam along
the sand as if expecting something to appear. The beam
catches Veronica emerging from the ocean, looking great in
a bikini, all wet and breathless.

PAT. Was it cold?

VERONICA. Yes.

PAT. Nice cold?

VERONICA. It was gorgeous. The kind of cold that reminds
you you're not dead. I needed that. God how I needed that.
*(On the next dune, Veronica starts searching among her things for a
towel, grabs one and starts drying.)*

PAT. Oh, I'm glad it was good for you.

VERONICA. Like swimming in chilled champagne. *(Pat throws
the flashlight to Veronica.)*

PAT. While you were out there, I thought of Bob. I sort of
miss him at a time like this? *(Surprised by the mention of her ex-
husband's name, Veronica casts the beam of light upon Pat.)*

VERONICA. Yeah?

PAT. I'm not saying you did wrong to divorce him. Just ...

VERONICA. Three's a crowd?

PAT. Now would I say that? No. *(Offended, Veronica throws the
flashlight back.)* It's just ... Bob was a real man, not scared of
an emotional problem.

---

* See Special Note on Songs and Recordings on copyright page.

VERONICA. Like me.

PAT. No. I mean, he'd be the daddy. Ya know? You could lean on Bob at times like this.

VERONICA. Unlike my brother.

PAT. I didn't say that. I couldn't be happier with Quentin but your Bob had less testosterone and sometimes that could be a relief. On the other hand Bob was cuddly and smooth, and sophisticated but also smart, in a mature sort of way. I ... I really miss Bob.

VERONICA. Hmmmn.

PAT. In one sense I'm glad you divorced him. He came on to me.

VERONICA. Whut...???

PAT. I knew I'd blurt that out someday and here I just did. Was that bad? Veronica? Veronica? *(Quentin enters with a blanket, a camping lamp and his attaché case.)*

QUENTIN. Hi! Sit on this.

PAT. Oh, thank you.

QUENTIN. She went in the ocean in the dark?

VERONICA. Why not?

QUENTIN. You say you're agoraphobic. You say you have vertigo ...

VERONICA. I also have guts. It was delicious. I floated on my back and offered my body to the stars.

QUENTIN. And the stars rejected the offer, I hope.

VERONICA. Yes, too bad or I'd be up there now, wouldn't I?

QUENTIN. Floating on your back. You could have wound up in Portugal. And you let her go in?

PAT. I'm gonna be the one person, in the history of the universe, who stops your sister from doing whatever she wants?

QUENTIN. There's no light for Crissakes.

PAT. There's the whole damn Milky Way.

VERONICA. This ocean will never be the same after tonight. So I went in, to taste it for the last time, the way it was.

PAT. Well there's always the Pacific.

QUENTIN. I don't understand a word you two are saying.

PAT. It's about your mother. Your mother. Bink! In the ocean. Like you put a tea bag in water, it becomes tea. You put your mother in the ocean. It becomes ... whatever. Your mother.

QUENTIN. You said Mom wanted to go in at dawn.

VERONICA. Don't be so nervous!

PAT. Honey, she did not put your mother in yet. Can't you stay still for a minute?

QUENTIN. *(Hands the attaché case off to Pat, takes the flashlight from her and hands it to Veronica.)* Your car trunk's locked. Let me have your keys.

VERONICA. What do you want from my trunk?

QUENTIN. Gasoline, fire wood. Anything ...

PAT. I'm roasting here.

QUENTIN. Let me do what I do best, okay?

VERONICA. Oh we have a real iron john here. There's only a beach umbrella in my trunk.

QUENTIN. Cut the routine Ronnie and just give me the keys.

VERONICA. *Quel* short fuse on this one!

QUENTIN. On the morning of my mother's "so called funeral" my fuse shrivels up like a dick in ice water. Give me the goddamn keys.

VERONICA. I'm to blame for what your mother requested?

PAT. I told you Bob would be different. *(Veronica uses the flashlight to hunt for the keys in her big black bag.)*

QUENTIN. It's not like my mother to wanna be dumped in the Atlantic "at dawn on August twelfth." Your ears heard that. Not mine.

VERONICA. Your ears were never there. You ran for your life, remember? Maybe she wanted us to experience the Perseid meteor showers.

QUENTIN. What did Mom know from the Perseid meteor showers? She didn't know the moon from a street light, our mother. *(She holds out the car keys for Quentin and casts the flashlight beam in his face.)*

VERONICA. Then why don't you just jump in your superfluous Range Rover and escape across the Sahara for which

11

the car was designed? *(He grabs the keys and the flashlight and casts the beam into her face.)*

QUENTIN.   I should drive an eighty-six Honda, like you? *(Pat has opened the attaché case and is going through his papers with mild curiosity.)*

PAT.   Guys.... Please don't. *(Veronica calls after Quentin who starts exiting.)*

VERONICA.   I'm a high-school French teacher, not a money-hungry lawyer who betrayed his middle class values.

PAT.   Oh God ...

QUENTIN.   Yeah, well this is all too romantic to be my mother. *(Veronica shouts after him as he goes offstage.)*

VERONICA.   So this was my idea? Maybe she was afraid you'd use her ashes to fertilize your lilacs in Chevy Chase. He's the agoraphobic one.

PAT.   Tsk. They're at the President's throat again. This clipping says a high school buddy "claims Bill Clinton used heroin intravenously in 1969 and that he gave three separate venereal diseases to his then girlfriend, Norma Schweers, syphilis, warts and genital herpes? *(Turns it over and reads.)* "The Onward Christian Soldiers of Fortune Review?" This has got to be a joke.

VERONICA.   Oh I don't know. Your husband's now a hustler for the Christian Coalition and believe me he puts out for those Pricillas.

PAT.   Oh stop with that stuff.

VERONICA.   I worship Bill Clinton. I would bare my breasts to him in a minute.

PAT.   I wish you wouldn't advertise your party affiliation, especially in front of the people who employ your brother. You're becoming a regular LaToya Jackson.

VERONICA.   Our parents were Democrats, remember.

PAT.   I hope you're not a Democrat just because your parents were.

VERONICA.   He's a blue collar descendant. What's this neo-conservative hoax he's perpetrating?

PAT.   It's called a job. Veronica what are you searching for in that monstrous bag, Sweetface? Maybe I've got one.

VERONICA. It's not that, Darling, Sugar-face.

PAT. You're digging so vehemently.

VERONICA. Angel Poop! I'm merely trying to find.... A Ross Perot button? Euuch, this is yours.

PAT. I never owned one of those.

VERONICA. It belonged to that Spinzio inamorata of yours.

PAT. Ralph Spinzio?

VERONICA. He left it behind when he came to Maine to chant with you? *Om na mah, Shivayha?* And then you fucked him in the cabin?

PAT. What did you just say?

VERONICA. I said it belonged to your old boyfriend Spinzio when he came to Maine to ...

PAT. Don't say it! Don't breathe it.

VERONICA. Well, take it. It's not mine.

PAT. Veronica, why's this stuff suddenly erupting out of you? He's coming. Put that back in your bag. *(Quentin returns.)*

QUENTIN. Those stars feel too close. I expect them to come crashing down on us any minute.

VERONICA. Republican catastrophic paranoia ...

PAT. Those aren't stars falling. They're only meteors, honey. But you know that.

QUENTIN. And I also know that meteors have hit the earth.

PAT. Well a beach umbrella will not protect our planet from a meteor shower.

QUENTIN. Do I look that stupid?

PAT. Yes. You look like you're in a Laurel and Hardy movie here. You're opening a beach umbrella in the dark.

QUENTIN. It's a *pied a terre* till the sun comes up. Den. Living room. The john's down the beach. I don't want to see the stars. They bother me.

VERONICA. Typical agoraphobic behavior.

PAT. I'm going to the john to chant.

QUENTIN. You chant right here. 'Cause the sun'll be up in a minute. I hate sand. It's morbid ...

PAT. Oh take your shoes off and enjoy it.

QUENTIN. ... all ground up fish bones and shells and it gets between your toes and pinches you in bed at night.

Where are Mom's ... you know. Looka me. I can't say the freakin' word ashes, her ashes.

VERONICA.   You just said it twice.

PAT.   Remains, honey.

QUENTIN.   Whatever they are, where are they?

VERONICA.   They're right there.

QUENTIN.   Where?

VERONICA.   There.

QUENTIN.   That's a tin can.

VERONICA.   What did you expect? A golden urn studded with rubies? This is what they came in. *(She's opening the can. He flies away from her.)*

QUENTIN.   Don't open it in front of me.

VERONICA.   Suddenly he's squeamish.

PAT.   Honey, try not to sweat.

QUENTIN.   Pat, sweating is not voluntary. Would I sweat if I didn't have to sweat? My pulse is going berserk here.

PAT.   Honey, take your shoes off and relax. *(Embraces him and sings.)* By the Sea, by the sea, by the beautiful sea ...

QUENTIN.   Don't baby me. When the sun comes up we'll say a prayer. I'll leave and you dump it, Veronica. You got me? It was your idea.

VERONICA.   You'll leave and I'll dump it?

PAT.   Can't you see what's wrong with him? He has too much feeling. You want his blood pressure to go through the roof?

VERONICA.   There is no roof. No floor, no walls. No law. No order. Sorry.

QUENTIN.   What is she digging for in there? Something morose?

PAT.   She's clawing away so ferociously, it's making me sea sick.

VERONICA.   Mother's spray cologne.

PAT.   Oh please don't spray that. I know you two have issues but don't work them out with your mother's cologne around me.

VERONICA.   If her cologne be here, could Mom be far away?

QUENTIN.   Put that thing back, Veronica. I'm not kidding.

VERONICA.   *(Veronica sprays it. A mist rises like a ghost before* her. *She continues spraying it in a circle around her.*) There she is. Hi Mom. Quentin is heartbroken over your departure. Talk to her Quentin.

PAT.   I swear to you, this girl's hard drive has crashed, totally.

QUENTIN.   How can she do that? Now that is ghoulish.

VERONICA.   Her glasses! Do you believe this?

QUENTIN.   Fuck.

PAT.   So stop her!

QUENTIN.   Put them back, Veronica.

PAT.   Cheesus ... *(Veronica puts on her mother's glasses.)*

VERONICA.   *(Spraying the cologne.)* Where is my Quentin? I can't see my little boy. Take care of your sister. She's all you have left.

PAT.   Breathe, honey. Like at the Zendo. *(Wearing the glasses, Veronica digs deeper into her bag.)*

VERONICA.   Oh. Get him outta here 'cause this will kill him.

QUENTIN.   What?

VERONICA.   You'll never survive this, Q.

PAT.   Turn your back to her.

QUENTIN.   What? *(Veronica pulls out an engagement ring with a huge diamond.)*

VERONICA.   For all intents and purposes our mother is here in my hand right now.

PAT.   Don't look.

QUENTIN.   What.... What is it? *(Veronica opens her hand.)*

VERONICA.   Mom's engagement ring.

PAT.   As if this wasn't planned. She's not in your hand. She's not in that can. She's up there. In the mind in the sky. Buy a book on Buddhism.

VERONICA.   I prefer the Hallelujah Chorus. I should go on the road with this bag. I've been shlepping it around for years. I grabbed it this morning only because it was black and here's this ring.

QUENTIN.   Let me have the ring for a minute.

PAT.   Don't give it to him. No.

QUENTIN.   I'm okay. Will you leave me alone?

VERONICA.   I would never deliberately put you through this.

QUENTIN.   I'll bet.

VERONICA. I never dreamed the ring was even in here.

QUENTIN. Let me have it.

PAT. No. Put your mother's stuff back in that bag, Ronnie. I'm not allowing it. He feels too much.

QUENTIN. I'm not a child, Pat. I want to see my mother's ring. May I have the flashlight? *(Pat throws the light and starts removing her panty hose. Handing the ring off to Quentin, Veronica weeps but it doesn't stop her from searching in her big black bag. Quentin examines the ring with the flashlight and he wells up.)* Mom. Jesus …

PAT. I'm sticking my feet in the water.

QUENTIN. Wait a minute. I think I feel her presence.

PAT and VERONICA. Huh?

QUENTIN. She's here. Oh my God, somehow she's here.

PAT. Goose bumps the size of goddamn golf balls you two are giving me.

QUENTIN. No. I do. I smell her.

PAT and VERONICA. *It's Shalimar!!!*

QUENTIN. Oh. *(Beat.)* I never saw this ring off her hand. It's a shock, you know?

VERONICA. Drop it in the sand and let's really have a cry.

QUENTIN. The woman's remains will soon be in the dark and violent Atlantic ocean and the most romantic object of her existence was nearly forgotten in a moldy old pocketbook?

VERONICA. Better than hocking it … like I had to.

QUENTIN. You hocked Bob's ring?

VERONICA. Bob who cheated on me, devastated my trust and divorced me? Damn right I hocked Bob's ring.

QUENTIN. You divorced him.

VERONICA. Yeah and he remarried in less than a year. You two think I just threw my marriage away. As if you remotely knew what it was like to live with a man who lies to you.

QUENTIN. That weekend after we were married the four of us went up to the cabin. Right?

VERONICA. Five of us.

PAT. Your mother.

QUENTIN. And you took Mom to a farm stand and Bob took you out in the canoe …

VERONICA.   Don't give me memories now, Q.

QUENTIN.   It's all we've got, memories and that tin can.

VERONICA.   Okay, so Bob took me out in the canoe.

QUENTIN.   And I looked up and said: God? Whoever you are, thank you for this blessing. My wife and mother walk arm in arm laughing like schoolgirls. My sister is gliding like a swan on the water with her prince. And just so the vision could burn in here, that night I sneaked down to the water and looked back at my three women shucking corn under a kitchen lamp. Ask any guy what it feels like to see the women in his life getting along. I keep that picture up here. Bob grillin' tuna steaks on the porch, and the three of you, shuckin' away and gigglin' like sisters. And you know, it was Bob who rented that place so we could be like a family. That's all he ever wanted.

VERONICA.   And I spoiled it by divorcing him? I didn't realize you were married to him, too.

PAT.   My engagement ring gets buried with me. Remember that, Q.

VERONICA.   Sweetie, diamonds cannot enter heaven. It's like putting tin in a microwave.

QUENTIN.   Where's Mom's wedding band?

VERONICA.   I'm wearing it.

QUENTIN.   Where's your own wedding band?

VERONICA.   I threw it at Bob. On Lexington Avenue—he was standing over a subway grating. Whoops, gone!

QUENTIN.   You didn't call the transit authority?

VERONICA.   I gave it up. You know, gold bands do not a marriage together keep. I do more to keep your marriage together than that gold band you're wearing.

PAT.   Excuse me?

QUENTIN.   How are you keeping my marriage together?

VERONICA.   By keeping my mouth shut.

QUENTIN.   What about keeping your mouth shut is saving my marriage? Veronica?

VERONICA.   If I told you I wouldn't be keeping my mouth shut.

QUENTIN.   After thirty five years of dealing with this hellcat my advice is, zone her the fuck out! *(Quentin goes back to examining the diamond under the flashlight.)*

PAT.   I'm too stressed tonight for witchcraft.

VERONICA.   You're not dressed like you're stressed.

PAT.   You are a starving lioness. I am a limping gazelle. I got the picture so back off!

VERONICA.   The funny thing is, Quentin, you haven't seen Mommy since Thanksgiving, though she asked for you, though she was sick and finally died without seeing you.

QUENTIN.   I have eaten my last guilt sandwich with you Ronnie.

VERONICA.   Where were you when the staff of that nursing home was ripping off every nickel the poor woman owned which is why she gave me her rings and since you're dying to know, I am "clawing" at this looking for a stale *Xanax,* because I haven't felt this displaced, this abandoned, this lost in the world since Bob left me. My Mother sits in that tin box waiting to mingle with that deep and violent ocean you so graphically described. And her Oedipal fixation can't wait to put on his golf shoes.

PAT.   *(Overlap.)* Veronica, I've got to step in here and order you to stop harassing my husband.

VERONICA.   Chant you. Like you did with Spinzio up in Maine.

QUENTIN.   Now wait a minute ...

VERONICA.   Look at her. She wears white.

QUENTIN.   What.... What're you doing here?

VERONICA.   Her mother didn't die. She has you. Something I never quite was able to have, through no fault of my own.

QUENTIN.   What didn't I give you?

VERONICA.   A Range Rover ... a big Tudor house full of down couches, and what did she do for this? She gave parties for Newt Gingrich's sister which nobody showed up for including the girl's brother. My husband's re-married, happily. I now live in a 1960's International style, mega-project, liberal, utopian apartment house with windows that open onto the crackheads of Washington Square Park ...

PAT.   And we worry about you all the time.

18

VERONICA. You think this is easy for me? I'm here fighting anxiety neither of you can even imagine. Why? Because my mother cared for him, far, far more then she ever did for me. Her favorite! Her Darling! My sense of safety, of mother and home are so poorly internalized because of you Quentin, that I'm completely lost wherever I go in life. I do not feel firmly attached to this world and now Mother's gone, poof! My husband, poof! The house we were raised in, poof! Our books, my piano. Where's my piano?

PAT. Hold her. *Hold your sister.*

QUENTIN. Ronnie, I can only advise you. I can't heal the hurt of your divorce. You need a mate. Someone to sleep with.

VERONICA. You advised me to go out and buy a king sized bed. I did. And what happened?

QUENTIN. You expect a man to knock on your door: "Hey, I heard you bought a king size bed?"

PAT. Quentin, just push through and throw your arms around her.

VERONICA. What good is that? And then you go and I don't see you for the rest of my life.

PAT. Did you see that? You didn't see that? It was huge with a tail like that. A huge meteor ... just shot down from way up ...

QUENTIN. I didn't see it.

PAT. ... and it landed out there in the middle of the ocean.

QUENTIN. Good. Let it be a sign that Mom is ready to follow that star. Dump her thing ... I'm sorry, empty it. And here's her ring. You can do what you want with it.

VERONICA. You wanted the ring. Keep it.

QUENTIN. No. You're the daughter. Mom gave Pat her diamond earrings.

VERONICA. Mom gave Pat. Wait-wait-wait. I thought I heard you say that Mommy gave your wife what?

QUENTIN. Show her the earrings.

PAT. Don't tear them off through the lobes.

VERONICA. These are one-karat diamonds that Bob and I bought for Mom. And look how she dresses for a funeral, like it's a celebration.

PAT.   Well I thought it was in a Zen sort of way.

VERONICA.   Sure. Now your competition is gone.

PAT.   Over your dead body.

VERONICA.   Give me back my ring.

QUENTIN.   I like the way she says *her* ring now.

PAT.   *(Removing the earrings.)* Veronica, I want you to … take these earrings, honey …

QUENTIN.   Hey. They were my mother's gift to you.

PAT.   There. Now give her the engagement ring.

QUENTIN.   No. Not now.

VERONICA.   He forgets who is keeping his marriage to-gether. And he is pissing her off.

PAT.   I have a premonition that if we don't get off this beach in the next ten seconds the entire Milky Way is gonna come crashing down upon me.

QUENTIN.   That's fine but I'm keeping this ring.

PAT.   Veronica, I got you the earrings. I'll get you the ring.

VERONICA.   You accepted these earrings from a woman you admittedly never liked?

PAT.   She never like me! She detested me.

VERONICA.   And that was your excuse for keeping him away from us?

QUENTIN.   Do you blame her?

PAT.   *(A near overlap.)* But I didn't. Quentin does what he wants to do. You don't know your brother.

VERONICA.   The problem is, Quentin doesn't know you.

PAT.   Oh Jesus, she's turning into Medea. Give her the ring! *(They don't notice that the light is increasing.)*

VERONICA.   There's an old Ross Perot button somewhere in here that someone left behind in the cabin …

PAT.   Veronica —

VERONICA.   You went to work that September and we were up at the lake in Maine and that Spinzio showed up.

PAT.   I'm history here. That's all folks. *(She treis to exit.)*

QUENTIN.   No. *(He holds her wrists.)*

VERONICA.   Remember Spinzio?

PAT.   Here comes the sky.

VERONICA.   She's lounging in silk shorts while *moi*, the

daughter, has to put on a hot dress every morning to drive Maman to *le docteur* and halfway there Maman doesn't have her checkbook ...

QUENTIN.   So what's the point?

VERONICA.   I have to turn around and watch your mother climb those steep cabin steps all by herself because Mommy never let anyone see where she kept her money. And what does she see when she hits the screen door?

QUENTIN.   What does she see?

VERONICA.   Spinzio's bare ass flanked by those two shiny knees.

PAT.   If you don't let me go now Quentin, I swear to God, I'll scream. I'm going to scream!

QUENTIN.   Let the oracle finish her story.

VERONICA.   She kept you away because we knew too much. That's the whole thing Q. Your mother caught them in the act. *(Veronica throws the Ross Perot button to their feet and gives them her back.)*

QUENTIN.   So my wife had sex with Spinzio that day? Is that what you're saying?

VERONICA.   That *week!*

QUENTIN.   But I knew that. She told me.

VERONICA.   Did she tell you your mother caught them doing it?

QUENTIN.   *(Lying.)* Actually, Mom told me.

VERONICA.   Mom told you she saw them fucking? No.

QUENTIN.   Oh cut this out.

VERONICA.   Look at him. Lying to my face. He knows I know he's lying. Why are you protecting her, Q?

QUENTIN.   I already knew about Spinzio.

PAT.   I don't need you to defend me to her.

VERONICA.   I know you're lying, Q.

QUENTIN.   *(Starting to lose it.)* Why ... are you doing this to me?

VERONICA.   She cheated on you, my brother, therefore she cheated on me. We've got another Bob here.

QUENTIN.   You two were like sisters. I don't get this.

VERONICA.   I don't need a sister. I don't want a sister. I need my brother. You don't get it. This is not about that one. It's about you. Wake up! Hello? *(He's stunned. Suddenly he starts to shut the umbrella and get his things together. His camping lamp, his blanket.)* What's he doin'? What the hell is this?

QUENTIN.   Ronnie, remember when we were kids how we used to pray on our knees every night...?

VERONICA.   Q, don't patronize me now ...

QUENTIN.   *(Overlap.)* ... For the past ten years I've been falling on my knees before this woman. I'm ... I love this woman ... more than any thing or person on the face of this earth including you, Mom, anyone ...

VERONICA.   Why? *(Overlap.)*

QUENTIN.   ... because she had the guts to tell me all that you just told me and more that you don't even the fuck know. Which is why she is to me, a million times more attractive than most women could ever aspire to be and believe me, she was beautiful to start out with. But her honesty made her something shining in my life ...

VERONICA.   *She betrayed you.*

QUENTIN.   *She shines in my life!* And I fall deeper in love with her every time she falls or fails so there's nothing you can tell me that won't make me *love her more.* There's more to marriage than a souvenir fuck from an old boyfriend. You'd still be married if you realized that.

PAT.   Quentin ... *(Overlap.)*

QUENTIN.   After you dumped Bob this woman was worried sick about your welfare.

PAT.   Quentin ...

QUENTIN.   We'd stay awake in bed at night trying to figure out a way to help you. You sent Bob packing for the same goddamn reason, one little slip and Boom! Overnight, you're the Pope, excommunicating everyone in sight. So, she fucked somebody. Who didn't? There are people fucking people on those planets up there. Horseshoe crabs are fucking in the ocean as we speak. She's good to me. I love her. So do me a favor and find yourself a new Bob. I have my Bob. She's my Bob and I'm hanging on to her. It's dawn, so do what you have to do. I don't want to be here for it. For me it's been over for a long time and I'm going home.

PAT.   Stay with your sister. I'll go back ...

QUENTIN. Stop making choices for me, both of you.

PAT. But you're her family.

QUENTIN. Her family is out there, a billion strangers waiting to meet her. God help them. I'm only her brother.

VERONICA. *Only* my brother?

QUENTIN. You scare me. I can't handle it.

VERONICA. I scare you?

QUENTIN. Please. Let me go home with Patti. Do not hurt us.

VERONICA. You want to miss Mom's funeral?

QUENTIN. *(Stunned.)* Yes. Yes. We're a day closer to where Mom went, somewhere up there. We'll all catch up to her soon enough.

VERONICA. Oh my God this guy's crazy.

PAT. Quentin, you're her last living relative ...

QUENTIN. I don't care.

VERONICA. You two are gonna leave me alone with this?

QUENTIN. You bet we are.

PAT. Stay with her. I'll drive the Range Rover. You two do what you have to do. She'll drive you home.

QUENTIN. I go where you go.

PAT. Not this time. The keys.

QUENTIN. Why are you doing this to me?

PAT. Because no one should have to do alone what you're leaving her to ... *(Do. Veronica is suddenly grabbing fistfuls of ashes and throwing them in a wide arc. Weeping loudly, she falls upon the sand mixing in the ashes and finally, falling upon them. In spite of her agony, Quentin is stuck, stunned, refusing to come D. to comfort his sister.)* Quentin ... Quentin ... *(Light is increasing unrealistically around them as the waves crash more rapidly and louder. Pat is stuck somehow, between Quentin and Veronica. The sun grows unnaturally brighter, the surf louder. Pat comes D. into the light, kneels beside Veronica and touches her back in an awkward attempt to comfort her. Veronica sits up and almost incomprehensibly, the two women embrace. The sun now becomes unbearably bright. A final wave crashes. Blackout. Music plays.)*

END

DAY

CHARACTERS

ACE — A man in his 30s
MACY — A woman in her 30s
BILL — A woman in her 30s

SCENE
A beach.

TIME
Summer; Noon.

DAY

Ace comes up over the dune, carrying a paper bag from a deli. He has small eyes, dirty blond hair, a developed body. Ace is sensitive, only moderately literate, shy, soft-spoken, and, for all his independence, he has a very low self-esteem. He is dressed in dirty no-style polyester shorts, muddy workman's shoes and a tank-top. His hands are black with ground-in dirt.

He stops for a moment at the top of the dune and looks at the ocean. He takes off his tank-top and wipes sweat from his torso, walks down to the beach, sits on the sand with great satisfaction and removes his shoes and socks. He opens the bag, takes out a sandwich and a beer. He spots a sandpiper, out in the surf, beyond our sight, follows its stiff-legged waddle across the sand with his whole head, making tracking, clicking, noises.

ACE.   So, what? You're a sandpiper, huh? So.... Yo! Sandpiper! How's it hanging? *(Beat.)* Hey! Sandpiper. Over here. *(Ace watches the bird a moment.)* What are you peckin' at? What is that, bugs? Surf bugs? Boy, people think you got it made, but you are *hustling* there, aren't you? *(He looks around, luxuriating.)* Oh, man. The sound of no human sound. Is the best sound there is. *(He looks back to the sandpiper.)* You would not believe the amount of *words* I've had to listen to in the last two weeks. You wouldn't believe there *was* that many words. Some people really like to hear themselves talk, fellow. *(He takes a bite from the sandwich.)* Just you and me, buddy. And that big ocean. *(Macy comes over the dune carrying a beach umbrella, a towel, and a lap-top PC. She notices Ace and moves toward a spot far away from him. She is a very good looking woman indeed; rather a businesswoman just now, wearing a skirt and long-sleeved shirt. To the sandwich.)* And for once they didn't forget your mustard. Lookin' good, sandwich.

MACY. I'm sorry?

ACE. Oh! No. I was taking to my *(Sandwich.)* — myself. I do that.

MACY. So do I. *(Ace reluctantly puts his tank-top back on. Macy gets the umbrellas planted in the sand; she struggles some opening it.)*

ACE. You want help there?

MACY. No, thanks, I have it. *(It closes on her. She yells to Ace from under it.)* Excuse me. Sir? Maybe you'd better — *(Ace comes over, opens it for her.)*

ACE. I got it.

MACY. Thanks.

ACE. No problem. Umbrellas one of those things can be — trickier than they look.

MACY. Very true. Thanks. *(She spreads a bath sheet in the shade and sits on it. He has started back; he stops.)*

ACE. What's the point of that? If you don't mind somebody asking.

MACY. Of what?

ACE. You come down to the beach, in the sun, then sit in the shade.

MACY. Oh. I like the beach and the ocean and the — solitude. I just don't always care for the sun. Not when I'm working. It's difficult to see the screen. It glares. *(She has set up her lap top, stares at the screen. Types a few words, smiles to herself.)*

ACE. So you're a writer?

MACY. What?

ACE. You a writer?

MACY. Yes.

ACE. I mean you could have been working on your grocery list, writing a Dear John letter, something.

MACY. No.

ACE. That's a lonely — occupation, huh?

MACY. If you're lucky. No, I don't find that. I've heard that, but I like the quiet time.

ACE. Yeah, me too. *(He moves back to his spot, eating his lunch, looks out at the ocean. She continues typing. Ace connects with the sandpiper again. Makes his traveling noises at it. She quits, glaring at him, thinking he's clicking at her. She watches him, curious; he's oblivious. She starts to go back to work, then she realizes something.)*

MACY.   Wait. I'm sorry. Aren't you one of the men doing the landscaping here?

ACE.   No. I wouldn't call it landscaping. Landscaping is drawing up plans, matching the colors or the textures or the something of the leaves and the flowers. What the guys and me are doing, we're digging holes. Planting trees. We're on our lunch hour.

MACY.   I see.

ACE.   An hour in this situation is forty minutes.

MACY.   It's looking great.

ACE.   It better, what he's paying for it. Oh. You know that guy?

MACY.   I'm staying here. I haven't seen you here before.

ACE.   Yeah, this is my first day in a while. I put in a lot of the plants around the pool last spring.

MACY.   You work part time?

ACE.   *(His motto.)* No, "I work full time on the days I decide to work."

MACY.   I mean I've seen the others here all week ... *(With almost everything she says she interrupts his lunch.)*

ACE.   *(Almost apologetic.)* I work when I need to. Or I work when I feel like it.

MACY.   You just call up and say, I feel like working today?

ACE.   Yeah.

MACY.   Nice work. If you can get it.

ACE.   Most anybody could get it. You just got to be willing to settle for it. *(Beat.)* Only I don't call. I go by Randy's place. *(A particular sore spot with him.)* I don't use the phone. When I was little, every time someone picked up the phone, my dad would say, that's five cents. Then, in a couple of years, they raised it to a dime, and I never used the phone after that, 'cause I knew it was only worth a nickel. So now it's like five times that, pay phones, so the phone companies are screwing it to you. It'd be different if some pay phone companies charged you fifteen cents and some was ten, you could walk on down the street and take your pick — you know, the free trade we're supposed to have with foreign countries, but not supposed to have here — but when they're all the same price, and all raise their prices at the same time, you know they're just ... like ...

MACY. Screwing it to you.

ACE. Yeah. So you got the choice of using the phone and getting screwed or not. So I don't use the phone.

MACY. I see.

ACE. It's nothing deep or nothing.

MACY. What do you do on days when you decide not to work?

ACE. Something else. Lay around. Smoke dope, solve the world's problems. Goof off. This spring I helped a guy build his house. It's very — occupying.

MACY. If you didn't work yesterday or the day before, what did you do? *(Pause. He just looks at her.)* Say, day before yesterday. What did you do?

ACE. I said. Nothing. Listened to a bunch of people talk.

MACY. What did they talk about?

ACE. What do people talk about? They talked about themselves.

MACY. Where?

ACE. Around. Why?

MACY. Just curious. *(A pause. He looks in his bag. He has put the sandwich back, takes out a pear.)*

ACE. Want a pear?

MACY. No. Thanks. *(He starts eating the pear. She smiles, continues to work.)*

ACE. You want half a sandwich?

MACY. I'm fine. Thanks. *(Closing the PC.)* I think you've got the right idea. This sun is too good to miss.

ACE. I don't want to interrupt you if you're working. I'm fine just sittin'. Don't pay any attention to me.

MACY. That would be pretty difficult. No, I need to take a breather. *(She spreads a towel in the sun and strips down to a very brief two-piece bathing suit, looking amazing. She spreads her arms to the sun.)* Oh, Lord. That feels great.

ACE.   Oh, my God. *(To the sandpiper.)* Are you seeing what I'm seeing? *(Macy rubs oil on her legs, arches her back, taking in the sun.)*

MACY.   Sometimes I have to literally remind myself to stop. And take in; experience the moment. Just let things come.

ACE.   Yeah. You want an apple?

MACY.   No. Thanks. I'm sorry to bother you. Do you think you could get my back?

ACE.   *(To the sandpiper.)* Oh, man. See, this is the sort of thing that doesn't happen to me. *(To Macy.)* I don't know, my hands aren't all that uh ...

MACY.   Just across the shoulders and the middle there.

ACE.   And the middle there. *(Self-effacing.)* My hands are pretty rough, I don't know ...

MACY.   That's all right. I like that.

ACE.   Oh, boy ... *(He goes to her, takes a bottle of water from her belongings, pours some on his hands, wipes them on his shorts. He looks up and down the beach.)* I don't know about this. *(He begins to rub oil on her back and midriff.)*

MACY.   No, it feels good. I get really hot.

ACE.   What did you say?

MACY.   Don't stop. I said I burn very easily.

ACE.   Yeah. Me too.

MACY.   *(Dreamily.)* So you've been listening to people talk. Where was that?

ACE.   Yeah, uh.... Over in town.

MACY.   What's in town?

ACE.   Well, you know. Buildings, stores. It's uh.... Town.

MACY.   I'm sorry. My name's Macy.

ACE.   Macy? Like the store?

MACY.   Umm. *(Beat.)* And your name — is...?

ACE.   Oh. Ace. Like the hardware.

MACY.   Ace? Ace. You don't get higher than an Ace.

ACE.   I don't know about that. *(Stops rubbing her.)* I think you're done there. *(Rubs some on his nose.)*

MACY.   Just a little more.

ACE.   Oh, boy ... *(Very distantly we might just hear:)*

BILL.   *(Off.)* ¿Son sordos ustedes? (Are you deaf?) *(Ace suddenly stops.)*

ACE.   Did you hear something?

MACY.   Mmmmm. Just the ocean. A sea gull.... Maybe ...

BILL.   *(Off.) Gracias por nada! (Ace is suddenly alarmed, knows immediately there's no place to hide.)*

ACE.   Oh, no. Aw, fuck! Oh, my luck. Aw, shit. Don't tell her where I went. Don't — Aw, shit. Man, you can't run, you can't hide. I gotta use your towel. *(Pulls towel from under her, Macy goes rolling.)* I'm sorry if I get it dirty, can't be helped.

BILL.   *(Off.)* Ace! You bastard!

BILL. *(Off.)*	ACE.
Goddamnit! What	Listen, I'm real sorry about
the hell do you mean,	this. You don't know me.
running out on me,	We ain't been talking.
I know you're not again!	Believe me, you don't want
What? I'm not good enough	to know me.
to be with your friends?	
What's that shit? You	
think I'm not sociable? That	
fuckin' tortilla trash are so	MACY.
special I can't eat with them?	I was just beginning to think
	maybe I did.

ACE.
Oh, great! *Now* you say that!
Don't think that. Maybe
some other time think that,
not now. Trust me on this.

(He hurriedly tries to erase the foot prints between her and him.)

ACE.   Oh, god. *(He situates himself as innocently as possible. Bill appears on top of the dune. She wears a short skirt, halter, high-heeled shoes, make-up—all askew, all slept-in several nights. A little high, strung-out, mental, on a jag. She runs her sentences together with abrupt shifts. A damn good looking woman in another life.)*

BILL.   Whatever you did to my Volvo, I know goddamned well you did, you're paying for it. Not another nickel out of me! I know your shit! *(Turning, yelling back furiously; no breath.)* Adam! You stay the fuck back there, don't drag after me like

32

some goddamned — stink! Go back to the fucking truck. I mean it. Why do you think I parked in the shade? Mommy loves you, honey! *(Back to Ace.)* What did you do to my goddamned car? *(Seeing Macy for the first time.)* What the hell's going down here?

ACE.   Shh. She lives — She's staying up there. *(Bill might cause a scene but she notices Adam again.)*

BILL.   Adam! You heard me. And leave those guys alone. Go to the fucking truck. I'm watching you. God knows what contagions that trash has.

ACE.   Don't call 'em trash. They're from Colombia.

BILL.   Stuck-up fucking wetbacks, wouldn't even look at me. I asked where you were, they fucking pointed. *(She comes down to join him.)*

ACE.   They don't know much English.

BILL.   I'm hip! Dime. Nickel bag, crack, ten dollar. That's why no decent people can get work here, fucking foreign aliens lapping up all the salaries; *that's* the Big Sucking Sound. All these fancy-assed matrons, dripping money, got to have their foreigners cooking for them. Too fuckin' cheap to pay white people. Cleaning up after them. Answering the phone, bastards can't even speak English. You know I know, too!

ACE.   You know. I mean I know you know.

BILL.   And don't try to tell me you didn't hear the truck.

ACE.   What truck?

BILL.   What truck. My truck. Me. You heard me coming and split. You chicken-gizzard piece of shit.

ACE.   Bill. I didn't hear the truck. I been waiting to come here all morning.

BILL.   What do you think that makes me look like, slopping after you in these shoes?

ACE.   If I'm gonna be workin' on the ocean, I get a break, I want to take advantage of it, I want to come over to the ocean. People pay millions to sit here. *(He opens the bag again, gets out the sandwich.)*

BILL.   I wouldn't be caught dead in this location.

ACE.   You want half a sandwich?

BILL.   You got a beer? I know you do! *(He gets one. She has found a joint in her purse, lights it, sits by him. He hands her the beer.)*

ACE.   Where's my —? Damnit, you chased away my sand-piper. *(Bill looks up and down the beach, no idea what he's talking about.)*

BILL.   You want a toke?

ACE.   Naw, I — *(He looks around at Macy, who pointedly ignores them.)* You shouldn't come by where I'm working. They don't understand.

BILL.   They? Who's they?

ACE.   The people I'm working for.

BILL.   Randy knows me.

ACE.   Randy's *clients*, that he has me working for. They don't want a lot of people around that aren't working.

BILL.   You took something out of my car so I couldn't start it, too.

ACE.   I didn't do nothing to your car, Bill. You couldn't get it started last night, I couldn't get it to start either. I'll look at it.

BILL.   The water isn't working in your shack.

ACE.   You gotta turn it on underneath.

BILL.   It's such bullshit living out in the middle of nowhere in a one room nothing. Like some anti-social murderer. I'm waking up in the middle of the goddamned woods. I don't know how I got there, I don't have my pills, I couldn't find Adam. You're gone.

ACE.   Adam was at your folks.

BILL.   I walked home, too, nobody would pick me up. These people are scum! Three miles, Ace!

ACE.   A mile and a half, maybe.

BILL.   In these shoes it's three miles!

ACE.   I had to go to work.

BILL.   Why didn't you wake me up?

ACE.   It was 6:30. I tried; move you to the bed. You were passed out.

BILL.   How'd you get to work? You didn't take your car.

ACE.   Randy picked me up.

BILL.   You took the *keys* to your car though! Count on that!

34

ACE. *(The law.)* Anything! I've told you! But you're never! driving my car!

BILL. OK. God. How'd you get to work?

ACE. *(Helpful, not angry.)* Do you hear anything? I said. Randy picked me up. Listen. Asking questions is just half of it, you gotta also listen to the answer.

BILL. You want a toke? You running the bulldozer this afternoon? *(He looks around, Macy looks the other way, Ace takes a hit on the joint.)*

ACE. Did you see a bulldozer back there? We're planting trees. That don't require machinery. I haven't run the bulldozer in two years; since I've known you I haven't run the bulldozer. You ask that every job.

BILL. *(Re: the joint.)* Not all of it! And don't put it out, roach it. And my folks are pissed at you. They want you to stop coming around. They think you're bad for me.

ACE. I couldn't be late for work, this is the first day I've been able to work in two weeks. I got this Saturday, this Sunday. Then I go back.

BILL. How much longer are you doing that stupid —

ACE. Come on —

BILL. What an asshole.

ACE. It's almost over. Don't talk about it.

BILL. Over. Shit. What? Does it make you feel like important in the community? Your civic duty?

ACE. Yes. It's something people do. You vote and you…. Don't talk about it.

BILL. It's ghoulish listening to that shit week after week. Where's Randy? I don't see him getting his hands dirty, planting those precious pine trees. Eating with that trash.

ACE. One of those guys you're calling trash is a doctor. Twenty seven years old. A what-do-you-call-them — pharmacist. He makes more money here, planting trees, than he would in Colombia, working at what he's got a degree for. There's six of them living in one room. All family, cousins, brother-in-laws. All from the same town. They send money back; then they all got a savings account here. They save everything. *(Beat.)* And they're Irish juniper.

BILL.   Who is? Bullshit. Irish juniper. They're illegal alien Colombians. Oh, fuck, you're talking about the trees. *(She leans against him.)*

ACE.   They're not pine. Prickly as hell. Don't pass out here.

BILL.   They look like those trees Van Gogh painted. When he was in the asylum. Down in the south of France. Arles. I didn't think they'd grow in this climate.

ACE.   They better. Cost six hundred apiece, wholesale. Takes four of us to get one of them off the truck.

BILL.   Cuddle me.

ACE.   Come on, people are —

BILL.   She doesn't care what we do. Excuse me, Miss? Do you mind if we cuddle?

MACY.   I beg your pardon?

BILL.   We might cuddle here.

MACY.   Be my guest. *(He does not cuddle her.)*

ACE.   Look at the ocean. Do you even realize you're on the beach? Bill. Look at the ocean.

BILL.   *(She looks at the ocean.)* I don't like it. I don't like to go to the beach. The ocean's — look at it. It's too profound. It's too — bigger than I am. And stronger, and deeper, it knows things. I don't think it's thoughtless. I think it's evil. *You* see the white caps and a fizzy surf or something, when you get your boat in the water, taking people out for trips, sail boats and sunsets. I just see — all the people who've gone down to their death; sailors, Pearl Harbor, the Lusitania, fucking Titanic. I look out like, it's just saying to me: "Bill, I don't give a fuck about you! You could jump off the boat, I'd take you down, I'd never think a thing about it. I'd still make the same flop against the side of the boat, the same surf sound. You'll never even have the satisfaction to catch me gloating." Only that fucker is always gloating. You know those cable-knit sweaters? Fishermen's sweaters? Got those braids down the front? Those got started in Ireland cause every mother knitted a different pattern so when her men folk drowned, got fished up all rotten, she could recognize his sweater and identify him. I'd never wear one of those; like wearing a body bag. The ocean doesn't take responsibility for its actions, and that sucks. Before you get all romantic about it, the ocean is just this hired hit man. Only hit woman. The ocean is a "she." Of course. "She's rough today." Boy...! You *know men* don't trust it. Anything they don't understand, scares the shit out of them, they call it "She." Evil piece of — *(Yelling out.) I'm on to you, bitch! (And for no good reason she hits at Ace, slapping his shoulders.)*

ACE. Hey! Bill! Stop it. I'm not the ocean. *(She quits.)* Are you OK? I got to go wash my hands off.

BILL. Don't leave. Where are you going? Aaaa!

ACE. It's twenty feet. You can watch. Come with me.

BILL. Don't leave.

ACE. I'm going to go wash my hands. Come on.

BILL. In these shoes? I'll watch.

ACE. Are you OK?

BILL. You're trying to make me crazy again!

ACE. OK. *(He moves off tentatively, seeing she's all right, then trots off. Bill feels uncomfortable, looks around. Finally she turns to Macy.)*

BILL. Hello.

MACY. Hi.

BILL. Would you mind if I sat with you? This sun is not my thing.

MACY. What?

BILL. My medication hasn't kicked in.

MACY. Oh. Actually I'm working.

BILL. That's fine. Forget it. I'm fine.

MACY. I'm sorry. I've got to get some of this —

BILL. — Skip it. Who needs you? It's just that I'm going to scream. I've been doing that a lot lately. It helps. Normally, when I sit in the sun I get a really good tan, I can palpably feel myself tanning, you know? But lately it just feels like the sun is bleaching me. *(She lights a cigarette, Macy has gone back to work. Flat statement.)* I know you, don't I.

MACY. Uh ... I don't think so. No, that's not likely.

BILL. My name's Bill. I mean not everybody calls me Bill. Some people call me Billie. I got this thing, facility ...

MACY. ... What thing is that?

BILL.   I never forget a face. Drives me crazy. *(Beat.)* Actually it's not so much the face, it's the whole thing, the whole person. Persona.

MACY.   I don't think so.

BILL.   No, I went to the courthouse yesterday. Ace spends so fucking much time there, I went to check up on him. With his luck the jury he's on will be sequestered the entire fucking summer. Boy, can he pick 'em. And I saw you in the back of the — what is it? Audience? Congregation? Anyway, I recognized you from school.

MACY.   You knew me at school.

BILL.   No. I didn't know you, I didn't give much of a shit for the political Radcliff riffraff.

MACY.   You went to Radcliff?

BILL.   *(Beat. Glares.)* They left the door open.

MACY.   No. I mean, god. Let me think …

BILL.   It's OK, we didn't run in the same crowd. What a stratified goddamned, uptight — talk about the polarization of the social classes.

MACY.   Tell me about it.

BILL.   The principle thing you learn in that hole is your place. In life. In line. Your stratum. What crap.

MACY.   It was very tiered wasn't it. I resented that too. I wasn't very high class, you might be thinking of someone else.

BILL.   No, *I* was very high caste. You were middle-middle. And what was it? Treasurer of the class? There was the Ridiculously Rich with Lineage, then the With Lineage but Not So Rich Anymore. Then the Unspeakably Trashy *"Nouveaus,"* then the Middle-Middle Political Worker Bees. You were what? Prelaw?

MACY.   That's amazing.

BILL.   I was just guessing, because I saw you in the courtroom.

MACY.   Oh, no. It's amazing you remember me. I was nobody. No, I'm a writer, not law. I'm writing a courtroom thing, mystery thing. Were you one of the Unspeakably Trashy *"Nouveaus"*?

BILL.   BAAT! Wrong! No, I was the ridiculously Rich with

Lineage. Go figure. Oh, how the mighty fall. Actually my folks — long story. You're new here or you'd have heard of me. Maybe I'm over estimating my renown. I'm probably yesterday's news. I hope to fuck. By now. *(Yelling.)* Ace! Get your ass up here.

MACY.   He's on the jury?

BILL.   Could you barf? Yeah, he's on the jury. Which brings into question this country's entire judiciary system.

MACY.   That's an important case.

BILL.   He doesn't talk about it.

MACY.   You have to have read about it.

BILL.   I can't really fix on anything outside of, say, fifteen feet.

MACY.   How did you get in? I'm sorry. That's a hard ticket to come by.

BILL.   I wouldn't know. Ace! Lineage, I told you. My folks have money — and this is America.

MACY.   This is the world.

BILL.   I hear that. Ace! I can't do this! She's talking to me! *(To Macy.)* Sorry. *(Ace comes trotting back. Macy tosses him her towel as he passes.)*

MACY.   Here.

ACE.   No, it'll dry off.

BILL.   What, are we sharing bathroom accessories now?

ACE.   Can't people even be friendly around you? She's staying with the guy who's property we're working on.

BILL.   That jerk!

MACY.   Bill tells me you're a juror on the Baker trial.

ACE.   Aw, for godsake, Bill.

BILL.   Well, she has an interest. She's political. She's from Radcliff

MACY.   That's a fascinating case.

BILL.   The man is a creep.

MACY.   Do you think? I think he's interesting. .

BILL.   He burned his house down, burned up the caretaker, I don't find that fascinating —

MACY.   Oh, the prosecution is a long way from proving he did it. And even so, he wouldn't have known the caretaker was there. I understood he was supposed to be away.

BILL. Which just proves —

MACY. No, they won't get involuntary manslaughter. I don't think they have much of a case for arson.

BILL. The man is a dirtbag and he's going to fry!

MACY. You're not being realistic. He's got money — and this is America.

ACE. Guys! Do you mind?

BILL. You are such a pain in the butt! *(To Macy.)* He's not supposed to talk about it . He's under caution.

MACY. I'm sorry.

BILL. It's his Civic Duty.

MACY. I thought you didn't know anything about the trial.

BILL. Try to talk about something else. They're gonna cook him, everybody wants a piece of it. It's a fucking barbecue. She's writing about it.

ACE. Aw Jesus. I can't talk to somebody who's writing —

MACY. No! I'm just interested in court procedure, not this case. Strictly basic research. I'm trying to write a crime novel.

ACE. You guys went to school together?

BILL. We were in school at the same time. Not together.

MACY. *(To Ace.)* Haven't you found it interesting? The case?

ACE. Yeah, it's — I don't know ...

MACY. I'm sorry, You're not supposed to talk about it. You have a boat. I mean, I couldn't help overhearing —

BILL. No problem. Yeah, tell her about your boat. *(No response.)* This 30 foot rotten piece of hull that he's been working on for two years, and is never going to —

ACE. We're gonna put it in the water next week. After I'm free.

BILL. He sees himself leading excursions out to some island for picnics. Anyone who would get in that tub —

MACY. But that's perfect. I mean for his philosophy. Self-employed, work when you want to work, not when you don't.

BILL. *(Looks at each of them.)* This, I assume, pertains to a conversation I interrupted.

MACY. I'm staying at the house here, he's working here, I asked him about the work they're doing. Does that threaten you? That we were talking?

ACE. Oh, boy.

BILL. No, I'm not going to get crazy. I am threatened by my glass of tomato juice in the morning. See that little cloud over there? The little puffy white one? Scares the shit out of me. *(To the cloud.)* I got my eye on you! Just don't try to pull something. *(To Macy.)* I'm out of the institution three weeks, if that cloud doesn't go away I'm re-committing myself.

ACE. Everybody doesn't have to know everything about you, Bill. Why do you say that? She wasn't that bad.

BILL. I wasn't that bad. I've been worse. I just get a little *visible* and my parents put me out of sight for a while.

MACY. I see. *(Bill climbs up on the dune, looking back toward the house.)*

BILL. Adam! Where the hell is he? I don't see Adam!

ACE. You told him to stay in the truck, he's probably laying down.

BILL. He's not lying down, he doesn't lie down. Adam! Shit! *(She charges off.)*

MACY. She seems incredibly hyper.

ACE. She's uh, one of a kind.

MACY. She was actually institutionalized?

ACE. No, her folks.... You know, she gets drunk, flips out, goes to the Clinic.... Comes out, gets drugged up, police bring her home, her folks put her back in the Clinic to keep her from gettin' arrested.

MACY. I'd think it'd be very difficult to stay with someone like that. *(Ace starts cleaning up the lunch debris.)* I'm probably way out of line saying that.

ACE. What? No, say what you want. Bill is — *(Beat.)* She depends on me.

MACY. Yes, they do. *(Beat. Brighter.)* You're a sailor, then. If you're rebuilding a boat. You like the ocean.

ACE. Oh, yeah. I mean, Bill's right, the ocean don't take responsibility for its actions. You got to know what you're doing. If something happens it's your fault, it's not the ocean's fault.

MACY. Ummm. But you like it.

ACE.   Yeah, that's — that's my — thing. That's where I'm good. Where I feel good about myself. Well, on a boat you feel good about everything. *(Beat.)* The idea is to sell this one, buy a bigger one that needs work, fix that up, sell it, buy a better one ...

MACY.   What's the ultimate goal?

ACE.   Maybe a fifty, sixty foot boat. Take people out. Stay around here till about November, take it down to the Keys.

MACY.   That sounds like a good plan. Motor? Or sails?

ACE.   Sail. I mean it's got a motor too, but it's a schooner. That's what I do — sail.

MACY.   I'm completely ignorant of boats. What do they run?

ACE.   Depends on the wind.

MACY.   I meant price. What do they cost?

ACE.   Fifty footer? Equipped. Good condition. Seventy-five, hundred thousand up.

MACY.   You're joking.

ACE.   That's used. You could get one for less, but a good boat, good condition, seventy-five to about a hundred. Brand new? Hell, two hundred probably to five hundred up, depends how fancy you want, depends who the maker is.

MACY.   Still, that's not impossible.

ACE.   You work up to it.

MACY.   That's no fun. *(Ace goes to the top of the dune, looks off toward the house.)* Did she find him?

ACE.   Yeah. He was laying down in the truck.

MACY.   Is she coming back?

ACE.   She's talking to one of the guys.

MACY.   I thought they didn't speak English.

ACE.   Bill's folks got a place down in Mexico. She's down there a lot. She just talks like that.

MACY.   So you're a sailor. With dreams.

ACE.   Yeah, "dreams" is right.

MACY.   No, it's perfect for you; you'd be great, I can see it.

ACE.   Well, like I said, I'm working on it.

MACY.   You just *look* like a captain of your own boat. I'd definitely go out with you. And you seem enterprising.

ACE.   Bull. That's one thing I don't ever want to be.

MACY.   It shouldn't be that difficult.

ACE.   What? Raise seventy-five, hundred thousand? Six years down the road, more. I got some saved up. Just takes time, that's one thing I got.

MACY.   Yeah, but you'd want a new one. You said two hundred? That's really not that much.

ACE.   Way out of my league. Some of the old ones are better.

MACY.   I've never understood that. Working that long for something. I mean when you could have it now.

ACE.   Yeah? How you figure? I could have it now? I get — *(He stops dead, looking at her. She holds his gaze.)* Oh. I'm pretty stupid, huh? What are you after? You're not staying at the house here, are you?

MACY.   Of course I am. Burt's an old friend.

ACE.   Yeah? What does he do? All these people Randy does their yards, spend a fortune, I never know how anybody got to have that much money.

MACY.   Burt? He's just a nice man with a lot of friends. Whom he's always interested in helping.

ACE.   Generous man.

MACY.   You have no idea.

ACE.   But not for nothing.

MACY.   I don't know anyone who doesn't expect something in return.

ACE.   Like what?

MACY.   Like — who knows? Not much. Like maybe a token favor.

ACE.   Two hundred thousand dollars, that's a hell of a token.

MACY.   But if it would save a friend from embarrassment.

ACE.   *(The light downs.)* Oh, man.

MACY.   Or if it would save a friend from inconvenience.

ACE.   Yeah. Or — what's the word? "Incarceration."

MACY.   Or that, of course. Or worse.

ACE.   I thought you said they didn't have a case.

MACY.   I think he'll get off. I didn't say how. It just takes one juror who isn't too sure. *(A pause. Bill comes back over the hill. She is much more mellow.)*

BILL.   Naturally the cute one wouldn't be the pharmacist. And naturally the pharmacist can't write a prescription in this country. Useless.

ACE.   You didn't ask him to —

BILL.   It was worth a shot. You're right, they're nice. The cute one is stupid as a post, but the pharmacist is bright. You know he's got two daughters? *(Macy starts folding up her towel, getting her stuff together.)*

ACE.   I know.

BILL.   *(Ironic.)* He show you their pictures?

ACE.   They're pretty.

BILL.   Oh, please. They're obviously going to run to fat by the time they're fifteen, but I told him they were cute. I think my medication must have kicked in.

ACE.   You can be nice when you want to be.

BILL.   I don't see the point in it most of the time. Why is that? Colombian men are gorgeous, the women are all ugly as Medusa.

ACE.   *(To Macy.)* You're leaving? That didn't take long. You've done what you came down to do, huh?

MACY.   Think about what we talked about. But not too long.

ACE.   I don't think so.

MACY.   *(Shocked.)* You what?

ACE.   I don't think so.

MACY.   Bill, you're going to have to talk some sense into your boyfriend.

BILL.   Sense? Short of a DNA transplant ...

MACY.   *(To Ace.)* Maybe once, maybe twice in a lifetime, an opportunity comes to someone ...

ACE.   Four or five times a day.

MACY.   An opportunity like *this* comes along ...

ACE.   To someone like me.

MACY.   To anyone.

BILL.   What?

ACE.   A friend of hers wants to buy me a boat.

BILL.   Why?

ACE.   I guess I'm in a position to do him a favor.

BILL.   And you don't want to?

ACE.   I'm not the ocean.

BILL.   *(To Macy.)* He's not the ocean. He's also very stubborn.

ACE.   It's just not something I can do.

BILL.   Oh. *(To Macy.)* He can't do it.

MACY.   You talk to him.

BILL.   No, you're asking the wrong person. If I wanted him to have a boat, I'd buy him a boat. But see, if he gets a boat, I'm afraid he'll take off. I mean I would if I had me hanging on me. *(Macy folds the umbrella with dispatch.)*

MACY.   You think about it.

ACE.   You handle that umbrella pretty good when you want to.

MACY.   You think about our talk. *(A beat. He is staring at her, she looks at him.)* What?

ACE.   You say anything more … I'm going to have to report this conversation. I'm sorry. *(Macy gathers her stuff up and walks to the top of the dune and turns.)*

MACY.   You really think you'll have your boat? Six years down the road?

ACE.   Yes or no. *(Macy leaves. Ace and Bill are standing next to each other. He turns and looks out at the ocean. She leans against him.)* Your pills kicked in.

BILL.   *(Seeing the sandpiper.)* Is that your sandpiper?

ACE.   Hey, buddy! You're back! *(Makes his tracking noises.)* Hey, he's looking at me. Fella, you are looking at one *stupid* human being.

BILL.   Don't talk. Cuddle me. *(He puts his arms around her, hugging her. Bill closes her eyes.)*

ACE.   Look at it, it's beautiful. You like the ocean a little, don't you?

BILL.   No.

ACE.   You'll go out on my boat won't you?

BILL.   If you tie me down. So I don't fall off. Stop talking. *(Ace looks at the sandpiper, clicking, follows him with his eyes across the beach. Not opening her eyes.)* Be still. *(Ace looks out at the ocean,*

holding her. A pause.)
ACE.   Lunch time's over. I gotta go back to work.
BILL.   I know. *(He holds her a moment longer, perfectly content, looking out at the ocean, as the lights fade.)*

DUSK

DUSK is dedicated to
Josephine Knight Jackson

CHARACTERS

Willy, Dana and Marsha are attractive people in their mid to late 30s.

DUSK

A beach at dusk. It is the end of summer. We are at the shoreline.

We listen to the surf a while. Just when we feel that nothing is going to happen, nothing at all, ever, Dana jogs across the shoreline. She is gone before we get a real look at her.

The same thing is true for Willy who now jogs across the same shoreline in the opposite direction — although he does slow down and look back over his shoulder in the direction of Dana.

Marsha enters. She has a beach towel and bag with her. She makes ready to swim.

Willy jogs by again. He takes no notice of her and is gone.

Marsha makes her awkward way to the water's edge just as Dana jogs by again. She takes no notice of the swimmer but we catch her looking back over her shoulder in the direction of Willy. She is gone.

Marsha puts her foot in the water. She reacts elaborately to the temperature and returns to her towel and beach bag and begins the ritual of getting dressed.

Willy jogs by again. He takes no notice of Marsha as he quickly strips down to his bathing suit and goes into the ocean.

MARSHA.   Hello. *(He is gone. Dana returns. She is winded and walking now.)* Hello.

DANA. Hello.

MARSHA. He went thataway.

DANA. Who?

MARSHA. Those. *(She points to Willy's clothes.)* The one who thinks he's a hulk. He did a little striptease for me, but I wasn't impressed.

DANA. I think the expression is hunk, not hulk. Hulk is menacing.

MARSHA. Speak for yourself.

DANA. *(Looking out to the ocean.)* He's a good swimmer.

MARSHA. Men like that usually are.

DANA. What do you mean?

MARSHA. Showoffs. He has the whole beach to himself but he has to strip down and go swimming right in front of us. It's the entire Atlantic Ocean but he has to choose these particular few feet to launch himself from like some sex rocket. I hate men like that, don't you?

DANA. Not really. It's a beach. It works both ways. Move on down the road.

MARSHA. I can't. I lost my car keys.

DANA. Oh. *(Marsha is looking in the sand for her keys but pretty soon she is looking through Willy's clothes.)* What are you doing?

MARSHA. Looking for them.

DANA. Those are his.

MARSHA. He shops at K-Mart. Do we like this?

DANA. That's terrible. *(Marsha sniffs Willy's clothes.)*

MARSHA. Very intense. You want to? *(She offers Dana the opportunity.)*

DANA. No! You can't do that.

MARSHA. It's not like I'm going through his wallet. *(She feels in his pants pockets.)* He doesn't have one. A man with no name and identity. A serial killer met on a beach at dusk! Not my fantasy, thank you.

DANA. Stop that, he's coming back! *(Willy returns from swimming.)*

WILLY. Hi, there, gorgeous.

MARSHA and DANA. Hi.

MARSHA. I'm sorry, I thought you were talking to me.

DANA. *(Overlapping.)* Excuse me, I thought you were.

WILLY. I'm not going to fight that undertow anymore. I don't recommend that you do either, unless you want me going in after you to pull you out. It's cold, too.

MARSHA. I know.

WILLY. My *cojones!*

MARSHA. I know. Mine, too!

WILLY. You're both new here. Welcome to my beach. I come here every day. Summer, winter, fall. Neither snow nor sleet nor rain keeps this beachcomber from his appointed rounds. This is my favorite time of day here. The beach is usually empty. You have it pretty much to yourself. And if you do run into someone, they're usually pretty interesting. At least they're more interested in their souls than in their suntans. This is my favorite time of year here, too. The water's still warm enough to swim. The really gross people have gone back to their rabbit warrens in the teeming cities and/or stifling hamlets of this sadly/gently, yet somehow-still-great declining nation of ours and only we, the semi-gross, for no one completely escapes the blight, only we three remain to bask in the last warm days of summer when the sunsets are like a golden blanket you can wrap around you.

MARSHA. That was very poetic.

WILLY. Thank you. I try. Some of the most meaningful relationships in my life have begun on the beach at sunset. At high noon on the strand, all you meet are people with a death wish. I'm talking about skin cancer. I learned my lesson the hard way. My doctor said, "Keep it up, Willy, and I'm going to be a rich man cutting the skin cancers out of you. Just keep it up. Me and my scalpels'll be waiting for you."

MARSHA and DANA. *(Wincing.)* Oooo!

WILLY. He didn't say that really. You have to exaggerate in life or people don't get the point you're making. It's not enough to say "I love you" anymore. You have to say it more like ten million times. I love you, I love you, I love you, I love you, I love you, I love you. Eventually, if you're lucky, and not hoarse or bored to death from saying it so much, they get it. "I get it! He loves me!" Of course by that time, you've probably moved on and are loving somebody else.

MARSHA. That is so, so sad.

DANA. That is so true.

WILLY. Where was I?

DANA. Love.

MARSHA. The impossibility of love.

WILLY. Skin cancer! My point is this: the sun, the source of life, is a killer. That's called a paradox. You don't look like ladies I have to explain what a paradox is to, so I won't. But I don't blush to tell you I didn't know one from a handsaw until Dr. Landeau started talking to me about those skin cancers unless I changed my wicked, wicked ways. I was a sun worshipper. I used to think a great tan was one of the three meanings of life. Don't ask me what the other two were. Boy, did I have my head up my ass! *Sur la plage* is no longer a safe place to be except at night. Or now. Now is safe.

MARSHA. Now is beautiful. Such delicate colors. That pale moon already shimmering on the cusp of a lilac/lavender horizon.

WILLY. Way to go, babe, way to go! You've got a touch of the poet yourself.

MARSHA. Don't tell Dr. Gluck.

WILLY. Who's Dr. Gluck?

MARSHA. My analyst.

WILLY. I figured. I hope neither of you object to being called "babe."

DANA. I don't know about her but.

WILLY. You mustn't take it personally. It's strictly generic. I grew up on Sonny and Cher.

DANA. Well maybe it's time you outgrew them. Cher did.

MARSHA. That wasn't called for.

WILLY. Thank you. Your friend.

MARSHA. She's not my friend.

DANA. Please don't refer to me in the third person like that. It's very dismissive. Thank you.

WILLY. Do you have a name?

DANA. Of course I have a name. Everyone has a name.

WILLY. What is it? I'd like to use it.

DANA. Never mind.

WILLY. That female of the species I mistakenly identified you as being with has a real bug up her ass.

MARSHA. I guess she does.

DANA. I don't have a bug up my ass. I resent you saying that. How do you know what I have up my ass? I was fine until she showed up.

MARSHA. Hi. I'm Marsha. I hate women like that, don't you?

WILLY. I hate people like that, period. I'm Willy. I mean, what's the big deal in talking to one another? Everybody's got some goddamn hidden agenda you're supposed to figure out. Life's too short. You are looking at a man without an agenda. What you see in me is what you get in me. I run about this deep. No, about *this* deep. That doesn't mean I'm shallow. I'm like clear Caribbean water you can see right to the bottom of, even at thirty feet. It just looks like it's shallow, but when you try to dive down to the bottom of it for the sunken treasure, Spanish gold or caskets of jewels you heard or hoped were waiting for you there, you think your lungs are going to explode before you get there. Sometimes you can't do it and you have to shoot back up to the surface for another gulp of air before you can try again. You want my advice? Take it easy. Take a real, real deep breath this time. What's your hurry? I'm worth the effort. I'm that piece of Spanish gold, that pirates' treasure, that king's ransom you've been looking for all your life. I'm right here. A good man is hard to find. I'm a good man. You've found him.

DANA. All right. My name is Dana. Are you satisfied?

WILLY. Dana, Marsha. Marsha, Dana. Dana, Marsha, Willy. We got us sorted out. So now what about this Dr. Gluck? Gluck means happy in German. Hell of a name for a therapist. Anything serious?

MARSHA. I have a poetic streak. If I'm not careful it gets the better of me every time. So I have to be on guard against people like you. But if we don't aspire to something higher than everyday talk we're no better than slugs. "Yo! Give me a beer." Anybody can say that. Dr. Gluck says that for some

55

people poetry is the enemy of truth. I said to her, "What about Shakespeare?" and she said, "Shakespeare wasn't one of those people, Marsha, but you are. Besides, he wasn't a poet. He was a playwright; you're a mess." Well, she didn't put it like that exactly but the implication was clearly there. I could hear it in her voice. It's called non-supportive therapy. It's the latest thing.

WILLY. You have wonderful breasts.

MARSHA. Thank you.

WILLY. Okay, your turn now. What can I do for you?

DANA. You can't do anything for me.

WILLY. Push/pull, push/pull, push/pull. Make up your mind.

DANA. How would you like it if I came up to you and said, "You have wonderful breasts"?

MARSHA. He didn't say it to you. He said it to me.

WILLY. I would feel foolish.

MARSHA. I don't feel foolish.

WILLY. Men don't have breasts you can admire half a mile away. We only have hearts and souls that you have to get up very, very, very close to us to feel.

DANA. I meant, how would you like it if I came up to you and said, "You have a wonderful chest"?

WILLY. I would like it. I would like it an awful lot.

DANA. That's the difference between men and women.

MARSHA. Speak for yourself.

WILLY. Actually, you don't have wonderful breasts, Donna, so I would never run the danger of saying that to you.

DANA. Thank you and the name is Dana.

WILLY. I'm sorry. They're too.

DANA. I know. Can we change the subject?

WILLY. You have a wonderful teeth. Terrific eyes. Great legs. Beautiful skin. A neck to die for. I'm not even going to mention the nose. I'm queer for noses. Noses and wrists. Don't get me started on wrists. But, hey, you can't have everything. Nobody's perfect. Look at me. I have trouble with names but other than that I'm a very nice guy.

DANA. It's Dana. Dana Mills.

WILLY. That wasn't so difficult, was it now?

DANA. I'm not in the habit of giving my name to strangers.

WILLY. Let's stop being strangers.

MARSHA. You can't just walk up to someone and tell them they have wonderful breasts and then just drop them like that, you know.

WILLY. No one's dropping anyone. You want to play with us? Get over here and play with us. Or do you want to sit on the sidelines and feel left out for the rest of your life?

MARSHA. I wasn't sitting on the sidelines. I was looking for my car keys. I've lost them.

WILLY. Do you know what the odds are of finding a set of car keys on a beach?

MARSHA. One in a million.

WILLY. One in ten million. Forget about your car keys, Marsha.

MARSHA. What am I going to do?

WILLY. Maybe Dana will drive you home.

DANA. I'm on foot.

WILLY. I'm on a bike.

MARSHA. Well, I guess I'll just have to stay here until someone rescues me.

DANA. You're probably wondering why I keep staring at you.

MARSHA. No, not really.

WILLY. She was talking to me.

DANA. I thought you were someone else.

WILLY. Who would you like me to be?

DANA. You wouldn't know him.

WILLY. Try me.

DANA. He's someone I was in high school with.

WILLY. I went to high school.

DANA. I wasn't suggesting you hadn't.

WILLY. So maybe I'm him. Don't stop. Fire away.

DANA. He was captain of the football team.

WILLY. That rules me out. I was the star quarterback but I wasn't the captain. Johnny Walsh was the captain of the football team.

DANA. I knew you weren't him.

WILLY. Sorry. I was the captain of the wrestling team, if that's any help.

DANA. I don't think we had a wrestling team but thanks anyway.

MARSHA. We had a wrestling team. I used to love wrestling. It was my favorite sport in high school. I loved wrestlers.

WILLY. Where was this?

MARSHA. Tunis.

WILLY. I don't think we wrestled Tunis.

MARSHA. Of course you didn't. It's in Tunisia.

WILLY. *That* Tunis!

MARSHA. I was a United States Foreign Service brat.

WILLY. It wasn't me then.

MARSHA. Who wasn't you?

WILLY. That good-looking guy in high school you never got over.

MARSHA. What good-looking guy in high school I never got over? I wasn't talking about any good-looking ...

WILLY. Everybody has a good-looking somebody in high school they never got over.

MARSHA. You're very conceited. First you were a star quarterback in high school.

WILLY. I was.

MARSHA. Now you're good-looking.

WILLY. I am.

DANA. You are. He is.

WILLY. Thank you.

MARSHA. And I suppose you can have any woman you want?

DANA. He didn't say that.

WILLY. I can actually.

DANA. That's the first really unattractive thing you've said.

WILLY. It's true. Any man can have any woman he wants. Any woman can have any man she wants.

DANA. I could have you?

WILLY. Absolutely.

MARSHA. I could, too?

WILLY. For sure.

MARSHA. Then what's the problem?

WILLY. There is no problem.

MARSHA. What about my car keys?

WILLY. We're not talking about car keys. We're talking about people. What makes people connect. What makes people not connect. Look, we all came down here looking for something. Maybe we found it. I don't know about you but that scares the shit out of me.

MARSHA. I came here to swim.

DANA. I came here to jog.

WILLY. I came here to meet two beautiful strangers.

DANA. Thank you.

MARSHA. You can't have both of us.

WILLY. Why not?

MARSHA. It's simply not done.

DANA. Speak for yourself.

MARSHA. I'm married.

DANA. I'm not. I'm separated.

MARSHA. So am I.

WILLY. I'm married.

DANA. But you're not separated?

WILLY. Not at all. I'm happily married.

DANA. Do you have a family?

WILLY. Unh-hunh.

MARSHA. Big?

WILLY. You might think so.

DANA. How big?

WILLY. Three boys and three girls.

DANA. That's huge.

WILLY. Not to me.

MARSHA. You seem so young to have so many children.

WILLY. We married young. Very young.

DANA. Right after high school?

WILLY. In high school. Our junior year. Instead of not getting over her the rest of my life, I married her.

DANA. Smart move.

WILLY. I think so.

MARSHA. And you're happy?

WILLY. Very happy.

DANA. Then how do you explain this?

WILLY. I don't.

MARSHA. This? What do you mean, this? There isn't any this. I lost my car keys.

WILLY. Dr. Happy must have his hands full with you, honey.

DANA. What do you mean, you don't explain this? Don't or can't?

WILLY. Don't have to, don't want to, don't need to. We're three lonely strangers on a beach at dusk. We have a chance to come together in some meaningful way. Whether we do or not is entirely up to us.

DANA. I think we all know what your definition of meaningful is.

MARSHA. Give the man a chance.

DANA. Anyone can come together like that.

MARSHA. Speak for yourself. Ignore her.

DANA. I've been coming together with men like that since my fourteenth birthday. And who are you to tell me I'm lonely? Maybe she's lonely. Maybe you're lonely.

MARSHA. I'm lonely, I'll admit it.

WILLY. Me, too.

DANA. All people are lonely when you put it like that.

WILLY. This is a golden opportunity, Mrs. Mills, don't pass it up. A golden opportunity to be 100% candid with another human being.

DANA. I'm not Mrs. Mills. Mills is my maiden name.

WILLY. Why didn't you give us your married name?

DANA. I'm known in the community. In case something happened.

WILLY. In case we made love?

MARSHA. I knew that's what you were up to.

DANA. I didn't want you going around town telling people you'd slept with Mrs. Ed McMahon.

MARSHA. You're Mrs. Ed Mc.

DANA. Of course not. Do I look like Mrs. Ed McMahon? It was a euphemism.

WILLY. So is slept with.

DANA. I hate the "F" word.

MARSHA. Me, too. I like "shtupped."

DANA. "Shtupped" is vulgar.

MARSHA. I'm not Jewish, so I wouldn't know.

DANA. I'm not Jewish either but to my ears, it's vulgar.

MARSHA. I just like the sound of it. "Shtupped!" What are you?

DANA. What do you mean? What am I?

MARSHA. You said you weren't Jewish.

DANA. Presbyterian.

MARSHA. I'm a non-practicing Catholic. You?

WILLY. Catholic.

MARSHA. See? I knew we had something in common.

WILLY. But I'm practicing. Very practicing. I took communion this morning. I'm going to confession tonight.

MARSHA. Let's hope you have something to confess.

WILLY. Not a shred of worry in that department. I don't believe in Evil with a capital "E" but I definitely believe in sin with a small "s." What about the expression "making love"?

DANA. You can't make love with a stranger. It's an emotional impossibility.

WILLY. Speak for yourself, Mrs. Ed McMahon, speak for yourself.

MARSHA. Yeah, speak for yourself. That's telling her.

WILLY. You are so wrong. Some of the best lovemaking of my entire life has been with an entire stranger.

DANA. Does your wife know that?

WILLY. Of course not. Why would I tell my wife something like that? Why would I hurt her or cause her dismay with a gratuitous recital of what happened in the parking lot just before I came over the dunes.

MARSHA. What happened?

WILLY. I made really spectacular love with a beautiful young woman who clearly was as physically and emotionally eager for some kind of one-on-one contact as I was. It was amazing. I saw her coming towards me across the parking lot. I'd just gotten off my bicycle. She had on shorts that were slit up the side, so I could tell that she was tan all over, which meant

61

that she sunbathed in the nude, like I do, and when she got up close to me she ripped my shirt open and started playing with my chest and I ripped her blouse open and started burying my face in her beautiful, beautiful breasts and before I knew it she had my pants down around my ankles and I pulled her shorts and panties down while she wrapped her legs around my waist and then we fell back on the hood of a car and the combination of the warm metal and her soft, soft flesh and my hard, hard muscle and what we were doing on that hot, hot car hood produced an almost instantaneous climax for both of us and before you knew it we both collapsed on the hood in happy exhaustion and agreed we didn't care if anyone saw us like this, including the town police or my wife or her husband, we were both so happy, so spent, it would be worth it.

DANA.   What kind of car was it?

WILLY.   A brown Toyota.

MARSHA.   That was my car.

WILLY.   Thank you for letting us make use of it.

DANA.   And that's what you call making love?

MARSHA.   Speak for yourself. That was a wonderful story.

DANA.   And that's exactly what it was. A story.

MARSHA.   I believe you.

DANA.   You want to believe him.

WILLY.   That's half the battle, Dana.

DANA.   What battle? There's no battle going on here.

WILLY.   There's always a battle when people meet for the first time. Who's going to control who.

MARSHA.   Whom. Who's going to control whom.

WILLY.   That's just what I'm talking about. Who's going to control who. Who's going to win. Who's going to break whose heart. Who's going to laugh. Who's going to cry. Who's going to live. Who's going to die.

MARSHA.   He's right. You're right.

WILLY.   There's a grand design to all this.

DANA.   What grand design?

WILLY.   There's a reason the three of us ended up at dusk on this particular day on this particular beach.

DANA.   So you can regale two innocent women with some cock-and-bull story about rutting with some local slut/whore on the hood of Martha here's car.

MARSHA.   Marsha. Cock-and-bull story! When was the last time you heard anyone use that expression? Cock-and-bull! And rutting! Where the hell do you come up with a word like rutting in the last ten minutes of the 20th Century?

WILLY.   Do you want to recognize the grand design in all this and proceed accordingly or do you want to thwart it and this encounter will have been as meaningful (or meaningless) as the last or next time you buy a quart of 2% lowfat milk at Handy-Andy or Piggly-Wiggly?

DANA.   If we can thwart it, how can it have been the grand design? I thought the grand design was something you couldn't thwart, even if you wanted to.

WILLY.   Then that's your grand design, Dana.

MARSHA.   She's hopeless.

WILLY.   I'm talking about change. I'm talking about seizing the moment. I'm talking about us! Being on this beach, the three of us, we can change our lives forever and ever, even if we never see each other again.

DANA.   That's the most ridiculous thing I've ever heard.

MARSHA.   So go. Leave. Poof! She's gone.

DANA.   You'd like that wouldn't you?

MARSHA.   As a matter of fact, I would.

DANA.   I don't know how to break this to you, lady, but he's not interested in you. It was me he noticed and kept turning back to look at.

MARSHA.   That was when you were still running. That was before he started talking to you. To know you is not to especially like you. You can jog your life away. It's your personality that needs the exercise.

DANA.   I'm not going to exchange pathetic insults with a frustrated woman no amount of therapy is going to help.

MARSHA.   What do you know about my life?

DANA.   The lost car keys! Give me a break.

WILLY.   This isn't the grand design I was talking about, ladies.

DANA. Shut up about your grand design. It's giving me the creeps.

WILLY. It's not my grand design.

MARSHA. Her grand design is to go home and alternately bore and annoy her husband.

DANA. My husband is beyond being bored or annoyed by anything I say or do.

MARSHA. I would seriously doubt that. Where there's a will there's a way. *(Dana has turned away from Willy and Marsha.)*

WILLY. What's wrong, Dana?

DANA. We were in an accident. A bad one. Almost a year ago. Arthur went through the windshield. I didn't have a scratch, of course. Arthur's a vegetable. I hate that expression. It's so coarse. I'm ashamed I've gotten used to saying it. People are never vegetables. He can't speak. He can't move. He will never make love to me again. It's not going to change. They told me he'll be like this for the rest of his life. He's 33 years old. I'm 36.

MARSHA. I'm sorry. I'm so sorry. I didn't know.

DANA. Are you ever so lonely, so achingly lonely, that you would like to walk out into that surf there and start swimming and swim and swim and swim and swim until you couldn't anymore and you go under and you finally take that one big breath that fills your lungs with water and do you ever wonder what it would be like to go that way?

WILLY. Who was driving?

MARSHA. How can you ask her something like that? What does it matter?

WILLY. Who was driving?

DANA. I was. I was. So much for your grand design. I don't see any grand design in my life. I see anger and despair and I see no relief for them. None. And then I saw a man jogging on the beach who reminded me of a lifeguard I had a crush on in high school before we moved to Ohio and I never got over. It's a small world, but not that small. Not that small. It never was, never will be.

WILLY. I did the same thing. Summer of junior year. The beach.

DANA. You had a high school crush on a lifeguard?

WILLY. Enormous.

MARSHA. You're gay. Now he tells us! Now you tell us. Goddamn it! Fuck, shit, piss! Fuck, fuck, fuck!

WILLY. Are you finished? A girl lifeguard. People project a lot of things onto lifeguards. When I used to sit up there on my platform I could feel all their wishes and desires being burned into me with so many hungry, desperate, needy eyes. It's terrifying to be the one people think can rescue them from their lives. Terrifying but wonderful, too. Some days I miss being that lifeguard, that object of desire, that 18-year-old kid too much. So much I don't like being who I am now. Somebody forgot to rescue the lifeguard.

DANA. You miss your youth. Everyone misses their youth.

MARSHA. Not everyone.

WILLY. I don't miss being 18. I miss feeling 18.

DANA. Let me get this straight. You were a lifeguard who had a crush on another lifeguard?

WILLY. I married her.

DANA. No wonder you never noticed me. I mean, no wonder he never noticed me.

WILLY. I'm sure he noticed you. You're a very attractive woman.

DANA. Thank you.

WILLY. Only the lifeguard he was attracted to was even more attractive.

DANA. Thank you.

WILLY. More attractive to him. It's all relative.

DANA. You're so wise.

WILLY. Thank you.

DANA. I'm being facetious.

WILLY. I know that.

MARSHA. Men don't like sarcastic women.

WILLY. Nobody likes sarcastic women. People don't like sarcastic people. Oh, maybe for a couple of years they do, but not for the long haul.

MARSHA. Why were you being sarcastic to him?

DANA. I think we all know why.

MARSHA. I want to hear it.

WILLY. There's sexual tension in the air.

MARSHA. There is?

WILLY. She thinks she wants to sleep with me but she doesn't think I want to sleep with her, so she's essentially hostile, and you don't think I know that you think you want to sleep with me, too, and so you're hanging around to see what happens, sort of like an eager puppy.

MARSHA. You're both lucky I have thick skin.

WILLY. Why do we need a defense against the truth? I think we should learn to embrace it.

DANA. Who do you want to sleep with?

WILLY. Either of you. Both of you. Neither of you. My wife. Or I could peel a grape. That's not the point.

MARSHA. What do you mean, you think I think I want to sleep with you? Maybe I know I want to. Or know I don't.

WILLY. Make up your mind.

MARSHA. Why should I? Either way I lose. You don't want to sleep with me. Nobody wants to sleep with me.

WILLY. Somebody wants to sleep with you. In this wide world, there's somebody wants to sleep with everyone.

MARSHA. Even a woman who has tried all her life to find someone she could really open up to? A husband who would listen, a girl friend who wouldn't judge, a parent who didn't reject? Her own children even? No, not them, especially not them. They'd be terrified if they knew who she really was. And if not terrified, terribly, terribly disappointed. Someone she could let all the barriers down with once, just once, and just be? Even a woman like that somebody wants to sleep with?

WILLY. We're right here.

DANA. What are you so afraid of, Marsha?

MARSHA. I wasn't talking about me. Why do you assume I was talking about me? I'm talking about a friend. I'm fine. My needs are met. I just want to find my car keys and savor these last moments of dusk before I go home and spend a well-planned evening in front of the television. We have a 37" screen with something called Stereo Surround Sound. No matter how loud you play it, there's never any distortion.

WILLY.   Look in your beach bag.
MARSHA.   What's in my beach bag?
WILLY.   Your car keys. *(She opens her beach bag and finds them.)*
MARSHA.   Well what do you know?
WILLY.   They have been all along. Can you admit that?
MARSHA.   No.
WILLY.   You can hardly see us in this light. You'll never see either one of us again. *(It is beginning to get very dark. The three actors will be isolated in pin spots but the beach will disappear.)*
MARSHA.   I'll tell my friend what you said. I'll tell her there's hope. That there is someone on this planet she can reach out to and who will reach out to her. I'll tell her I met her guardian angel on the beach. An extremely good-looking former lifeguard guardian angel. I think the irony of that will amuse her.
WILLY.   Pretty soon it will be dark and we won't be able to see each other anymore. We'll be three voices in the dark with nothing but the sound of the waves to comfort and console us. I'm sorry about your husband, Dana. I'm sorry about your friend, Marsha.
MARSHA.   Thank you.
WILLY.   I'm sorry I wasn't your lifeguard.
DANA.   I'm sorry, too.
MARSHA.   Don't you have to go home for supper?
WILLY.   Oh sure. We're having swordfish.
MARSHA.   They'll all be wondering what happened to me.
DANA.   I told them I'd be back in 20 minutes. I can hear them now.
MARSHA.   Is that a boat out there?
DANA.   Where?
MARSHA.   There.
DANA.   I can't see where you're pointing.
WILLY.   It's a fishing boat.
DANA.   Where? Oh, there. I see it.
WILLY.   We could be fishermen. The three of us. Our whole lives spent on the sea, looking back at the land, never inhabiting it, except on holidays. Christmas, Thanksgiving.
MARSHA.   That's my favorite. No stress. Christmas is very stressful.

DANA.   I would never come ashore. Christmas, New Year's, never. Just float and float and float.
MARSHA.   I can't move.
WILLY.   Sometimes I spend the whole night here just staring out to sea, listening to the waves, trying to count the stars.
DANA.   Nobody can count the stars.
MARSHA.   I told a lie. Nobody'll be wondering what happened to me. And I knew the car keys were in my beach bag.
DANA.   We knew that.
WILLY.   I didn't.
MARSHA.   That sound. Nothing matters next to it.
WILLY.   It's life. Just life.
DANA.   Ssshh, I'm trying to listen. *(By now the stage is totally dark. We cannot see the three of them. All we hear is the sound of the waves.)*

THE END

PROPERTY LIST

DAWN
Flashlight (PAT)
Black bag (VERONICA) with:
      car keys
      Ross Perot campaign button
      eyeglasses
      bottle of spray cologne
      engagement ring
Towel (PAT)
Blanket (QUENTIN)
Camp light (QUENTIN)
Attaché case with papers (QUENTIN)
Tin can with ashes (VERONICA)
Panty hose (PAT)
Diamond earrings (PAT)

DAY
Paper bag from deli (ACE) with:
      sandwich
      beer
      pear
Beach umbrella (MACY)
Towel (MACY)
Lap-top computer (MACY)
Bath sheet (MACY)
Sun bathing oil (MACY)
Bottle of water (MACY)
Purse (BILL) with:
      joint
Cigarette (BILL)
Lighter or matches (BILL)

DUSK
Beach towel (MARSHA)
Beach bag (MARSHA) with:
     car keys